AF476966

ArT RANDOM

KYOTO SHOIN

First published in Japan 1991 by KYOTO SHOIN INTERNATIONAL Co., Ltd.
Sanjo agaru, Horikawa, Nakagyo-ku, Kyoto, Japan. TEL[075]841-9123

Editorial director : Kyoichi Tsuzuki
Art director : Ichiro Miyagawa

© Copyright 1991 : Adam Lowe

All reproductions by courtesy of the artist.

ISBN4-7636-8578-3 C0371 P1980E

Printed and bound in Kyoto by SHASHIN KAGAKU Co., Ltd.

Adam Lowe is represented by The Pomeroy Purdy Gallery, London.

Adam Lowe

Transfer Paintings 1990
Surface Mapping 1991

Surface Mapping 1991

A series of five prints published by The Print Centre, London.

The five prints which form this series are literally maps made from the surface of five paintings. The paintings, made expressly for this purpose, have a highly developed use of texture where the qualities of the paint are as important as its colour or compositional role. The paint is applied both directly and indirectly using brushes, silk screen and various transfer techniques in order to extend the spatial and textural possibilities within the painting. An area of the blue can appear to change colour, becoming matt or gloss depending on the way the light is reflected or absorbed.

From the surface of each painting a silicon mould was made which was then cast into a uniformly thin layer of fibreglass. This fibreglass sheet was then inked-up and printed as a two colour intaglio print. Marks that are hardly visible on the painting become focal points in the prints and attention is concentrated on the way spatial representations emerge from a mass of brushstrokes, marks and textures. A substantial amount of experimentation and research was necessary before an approach was found which elevated these qualities into the subject of the work. The result is a series of maps which allow a number of responses to be projected onto them.

表層図　1991

5枚のプリントによるシリーズ、ロンドン、ザ・プリント・センター

5枚のプリントからなるこのシリーズは、5枚のペインティングから制作され、文字どおりの地図である。5枚のペインティングはこの目的のために特別に制作されたものであり、絵の具の質そのものが色彩や画面構成の役割同様に重要であるような、質感の強調にその力点が置かれている。絵の具は絵筆、シルクスクリーン、その他様々な技法によって直接、また間接的に画面に置かれ、画面内の空間および質感の可能性を拡大することを狙っている。たとえば青の部分はその色も変わりうるし、また艶消しや光沢にも光の反射や吸収の具合によって変わっていく。

それぞれのペインティングからはシリコンによる型が取られ、そこから一定の薄さのファイバーグラスの型が作られる。こうして出来たファイバーグラスのシートは2色のインキに着色されて、インタリオ（凸版）プリントとして刷り上がる。ペインティングではほとんど見えなかった痕跡がこのプリントでは焦点となり、画面上の筆跡や質感などの総体から浮がび上がる空間的表現に、注意が集中するようになる。実に多くの実験とリサーチが、このような画面感覚を作品の主題としうるこのアプローチの発見には必要であった。そして結果として出来上がったのが、様々な反応を引き起こしうる一連の地図というわけである。

Portfolio fabrication: Peter Fleissig
Photography: John Jones Ltd.
All prints are printed on 400gsm. Arches paper
The dimensions are 90 x 120 cms.

1991

ALL SETS ARE IN AN EDITION OF FIVE SIGNED AND NUMBERED COPIES. PRINTED FROM RESIN PLATES ON SHEETS OF 400 GRAM ARCHES PAPER. PUBLISHED BY THE PRINT CENTRE LONDON. FABRICATION © PETER FLEISSIG COPYRIGHT © ADAM LOWE

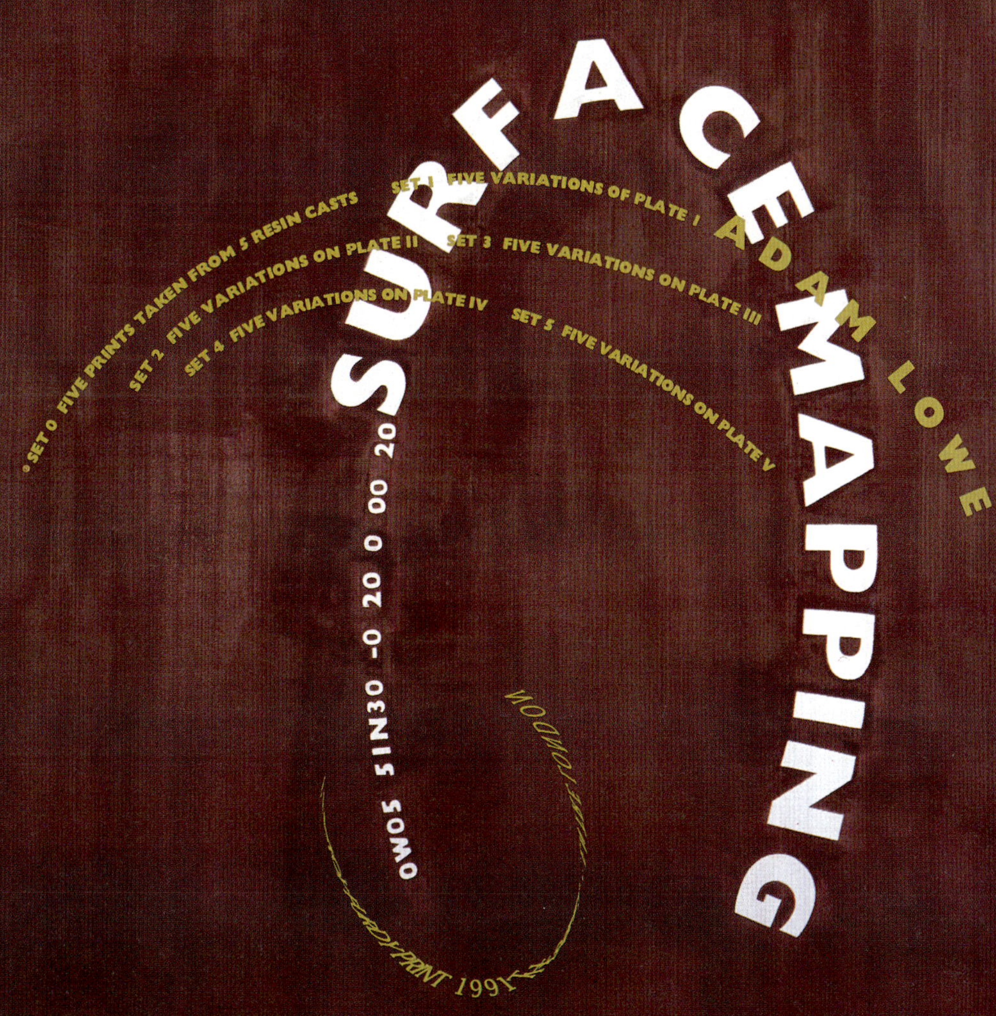

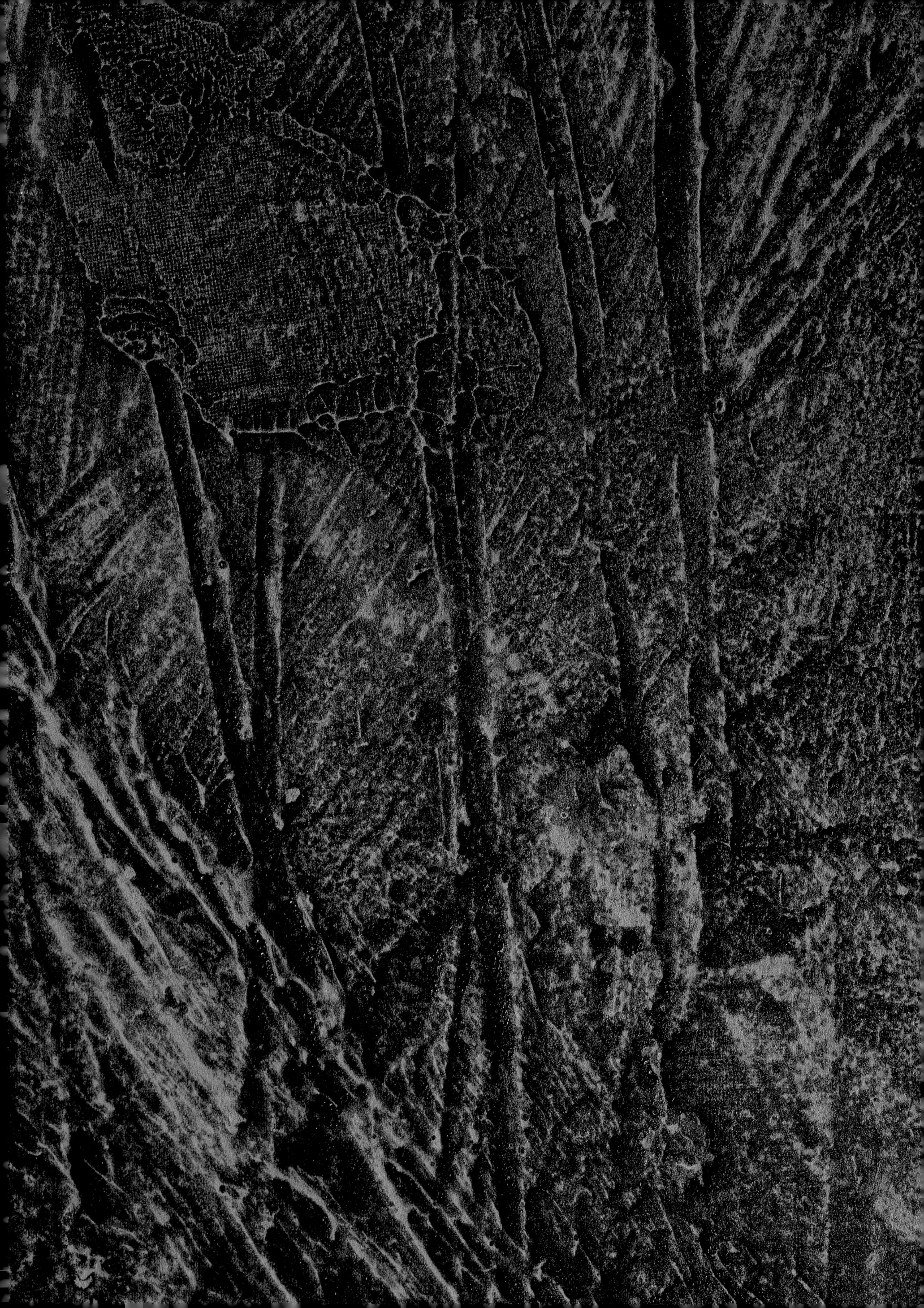

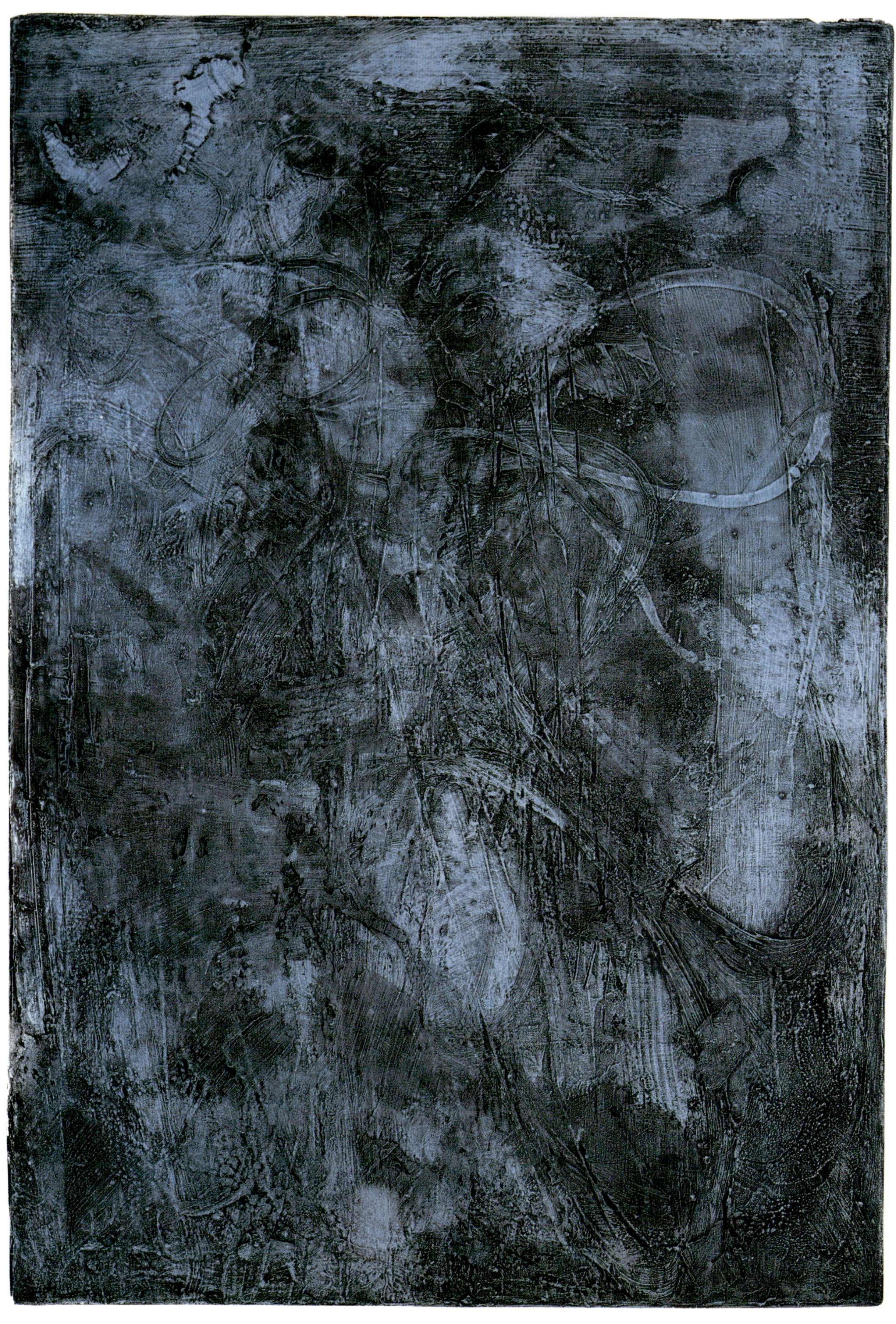

Surface Mapping I
opposite detail

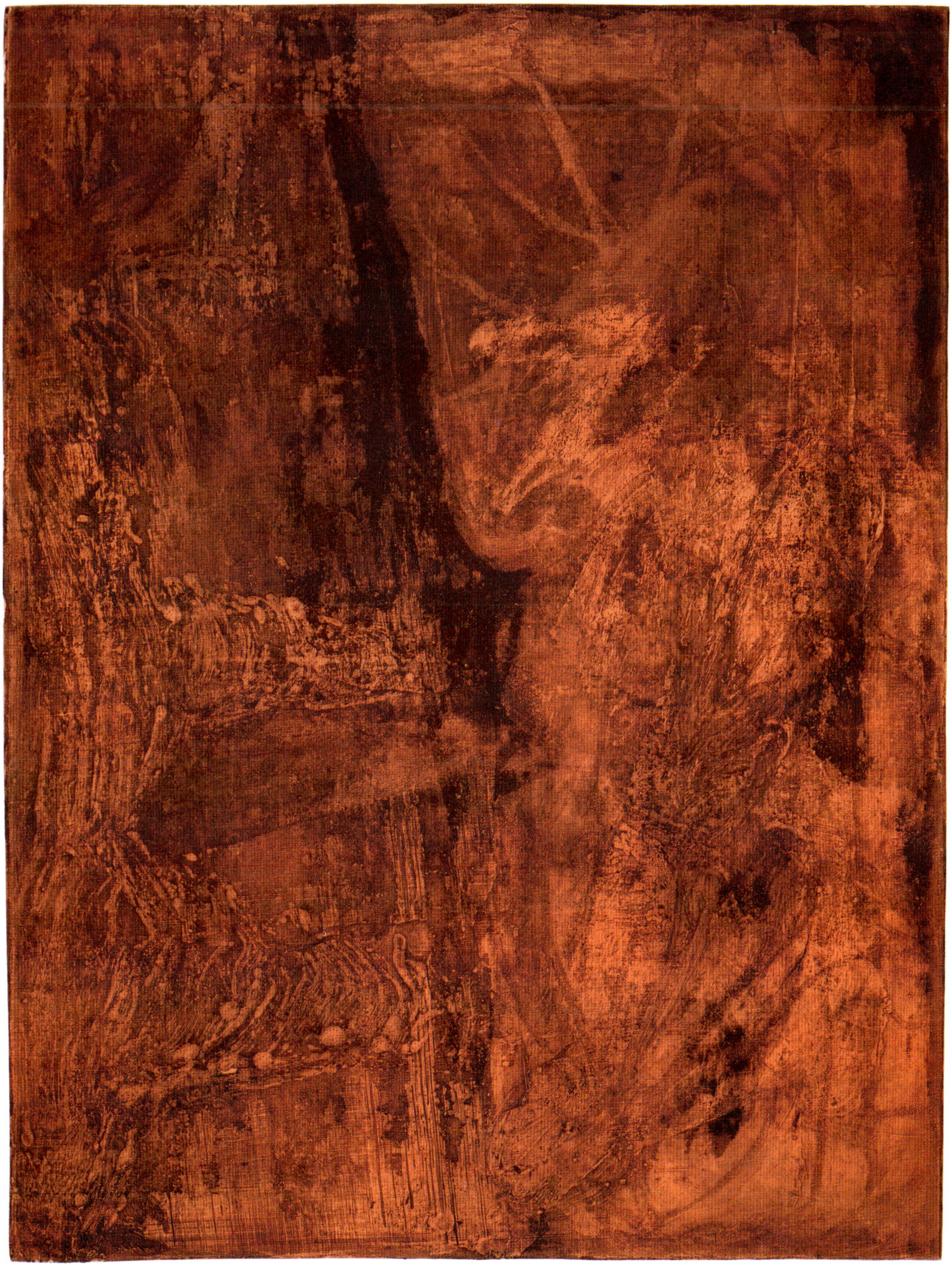

Surface Mapping II
opposite: detail

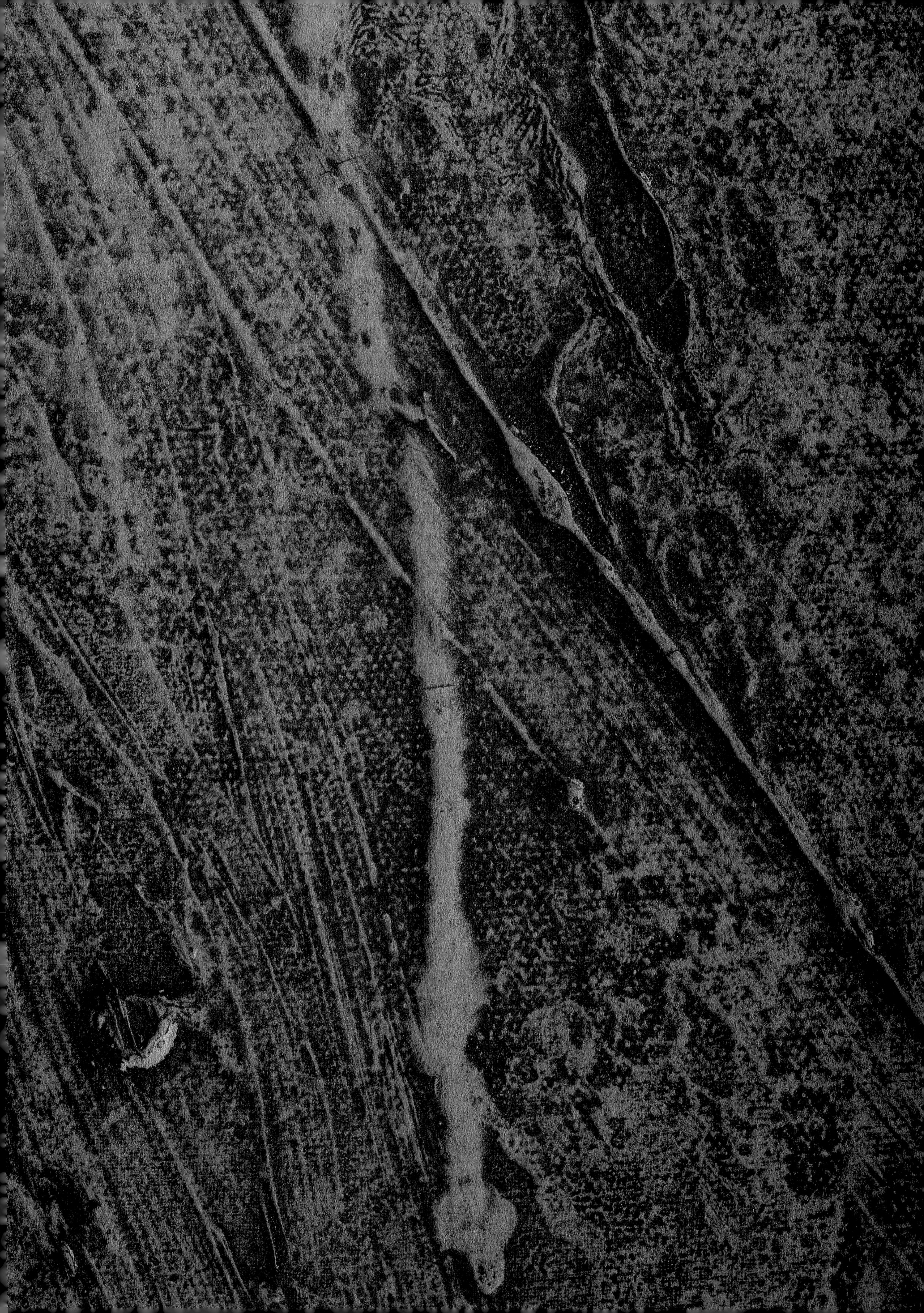

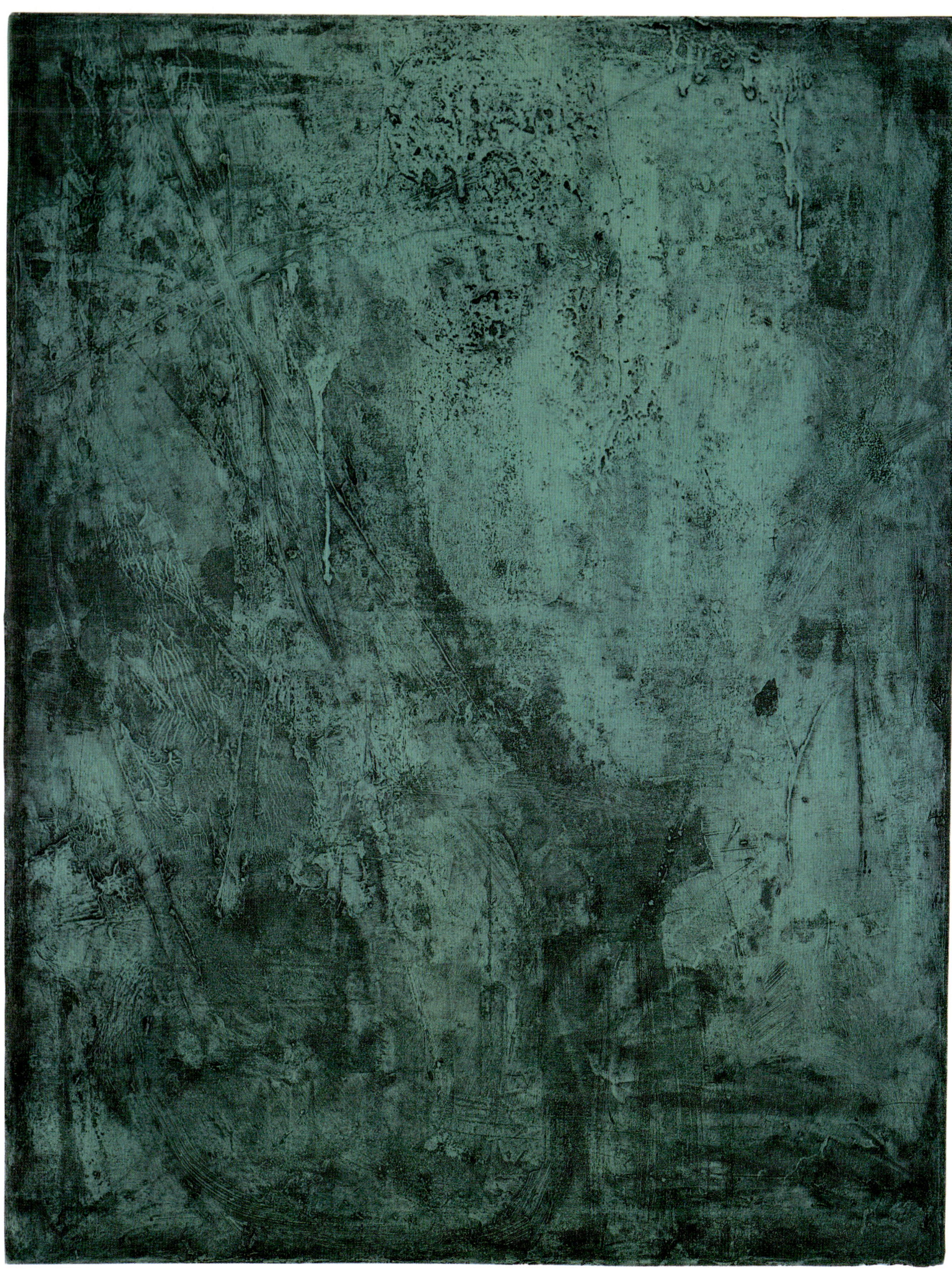

Surface Mapping III
opposite: detail

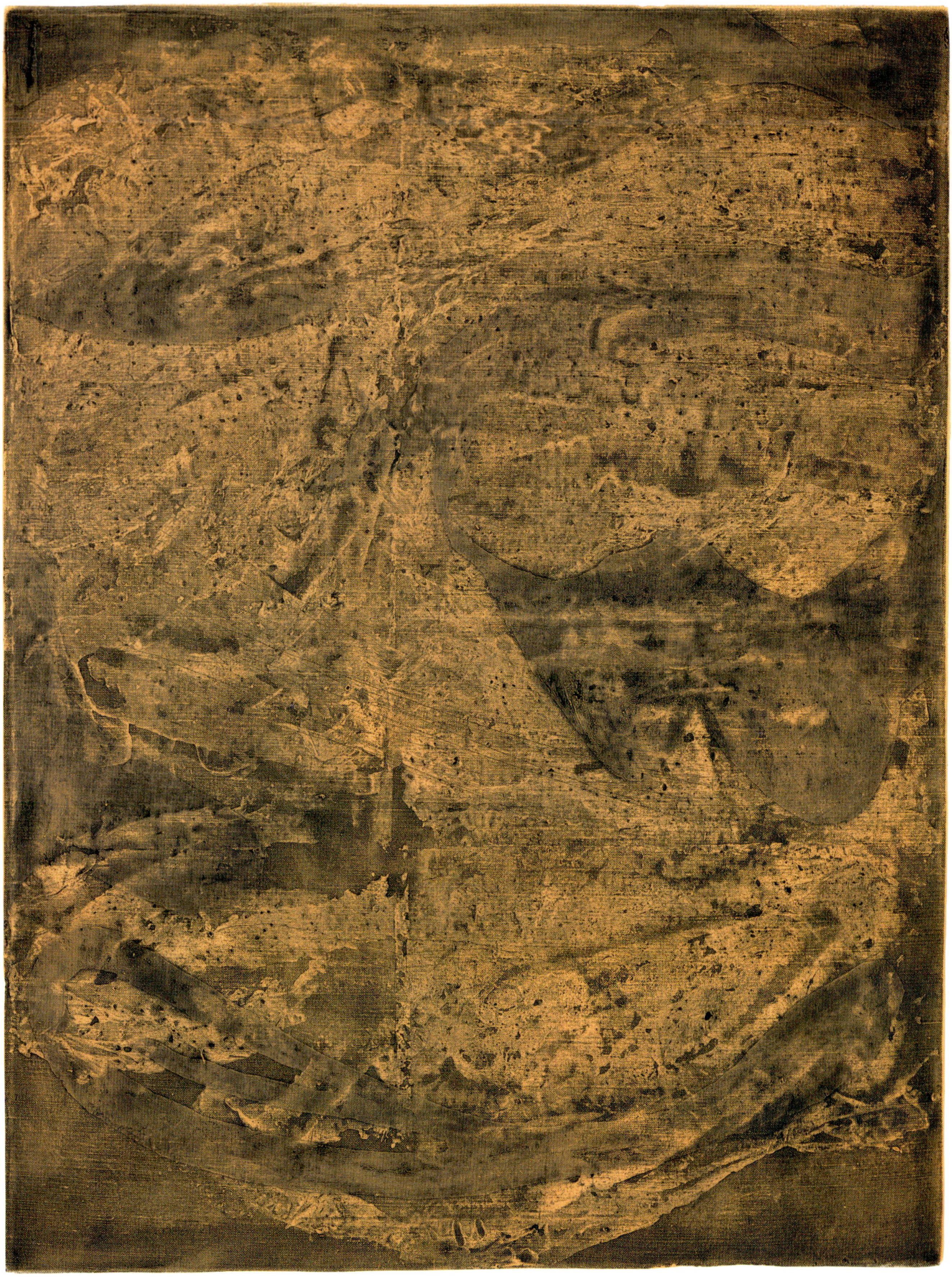

Surface Mapping IV
opposite: detail

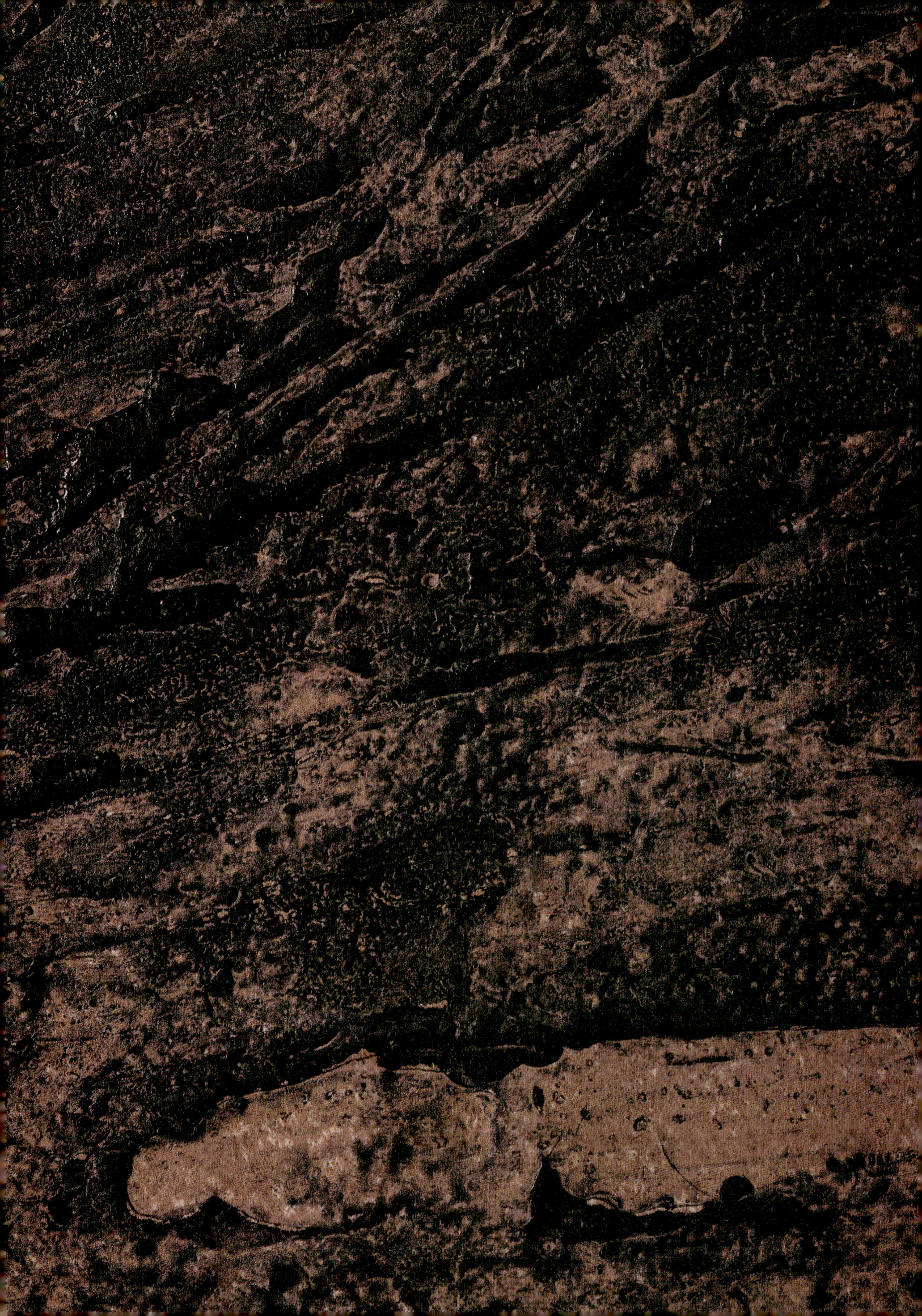

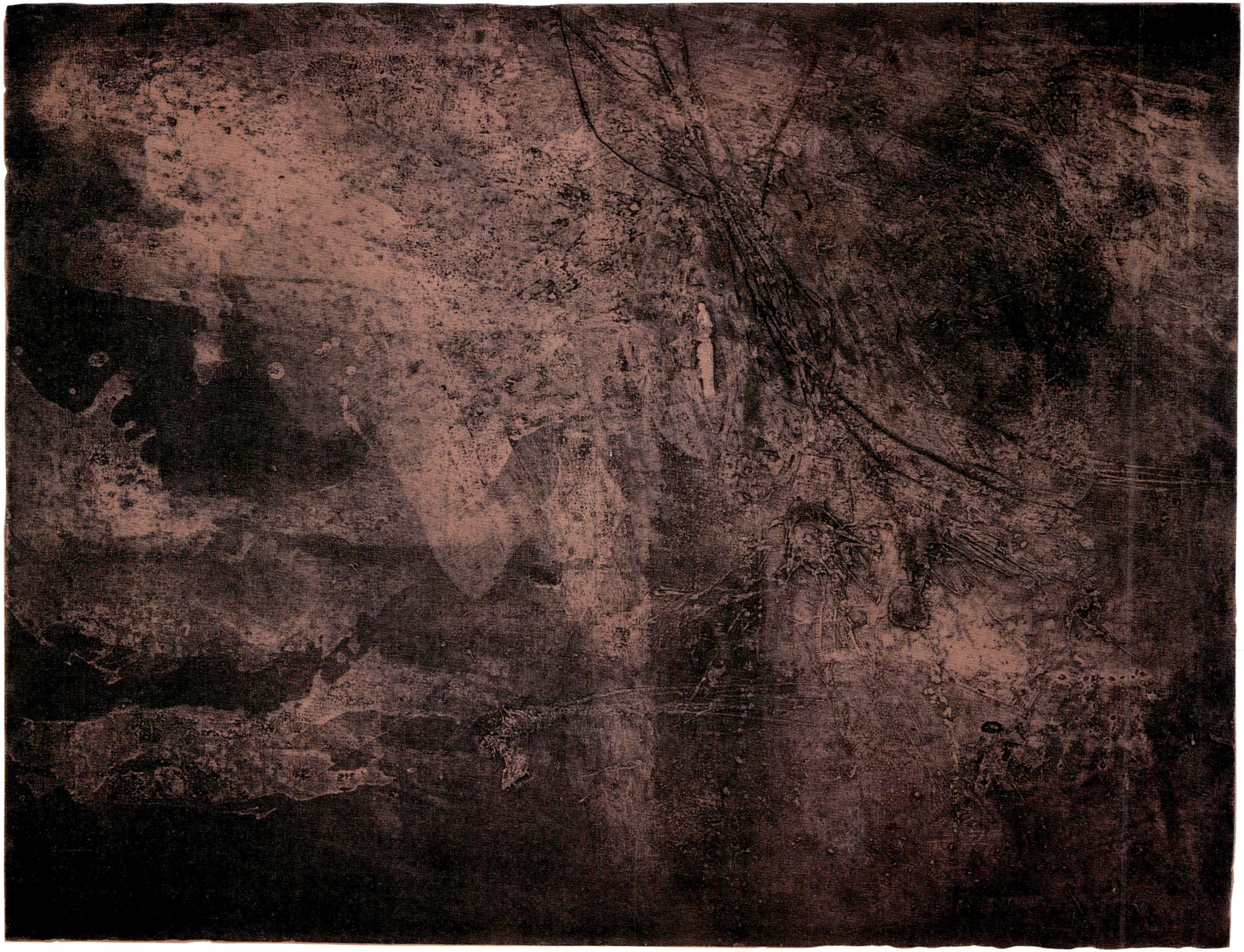

Surface Mapping V
opposite: detail

Transfer Paintings

These paintings are grouped together under a descriptive title which refers to the process by which they were made. The paint is applied using a gum coated, water soluble, transfer paper. It is the inter-action between the oil paint and the water which gives them the particular qualities they possess. This process allows both a conceptual distance and a directness while, in accordance with many of the tenets of surrealism, generating possibilities that are impossible to preconceive. The procedure facilitates a wide range of spatial possibilities and allows wet paint to be layered over wet paint without the colours mixing. The application can be thick and opaque or thin transparent skins of paint can float over the surface. Gestures and marks can be 'rehearsed' before being applied to the surface of the painting allowing a form of visual improvisation to take place. These are referential images but they do not rely on mimetic illusions of space, neither landscape nor entirely abstract they inhabit a mental space where the barriers between things are flexible and images can metamorphose without anything seeming out of place.

転写によるペインティング

ポレンサ、マルヨカ、1990

この一連のペインティングは、制作のプロセスを示す説明的なタイトルのもとにまとめられている。つまりゴム引きされた、水溶性の転写紙をつかって絵の具が置かれているのである。油絵の具と水との相互影響によって、それぞれの独特な性質があらわになる。このプロセスはコンセプチュアルな距離感と直接性とを同時に得られるだけでなく、予期することの不可能な可能性を引き起こす、シュールレアリズムの概念とも調和するものである。この過程によってさまざまな空間的可能性が助長されるようになり、また乾かない絵の具を幾層も色の交じり合うことなしに重ねていけるようになる。素材は厚く不透明でもかまわないし、薄く透明感のある絵の具を表面に浮き上がせれることも出来る。実際に画面に置かれる前に動きや筆捌きを「リハーサル」できるということによって、ある種の視覚的即興が可能になる。これらはなにかを指し示すイメージであるとはいえ、疑似的な空間の錯覚でもなければ風景でもまったくの抽象でもなく、それは事物の境界が曖昧になり、イメージがなんの違和感もなく変容していけるような、精神空間にあるものである。

Photography: Edward Woodman
The following works all measure 61 x 91 cms., oil on board

Transfer Paintings
1990
Pollensa Mallorca

Transfer Painting 1

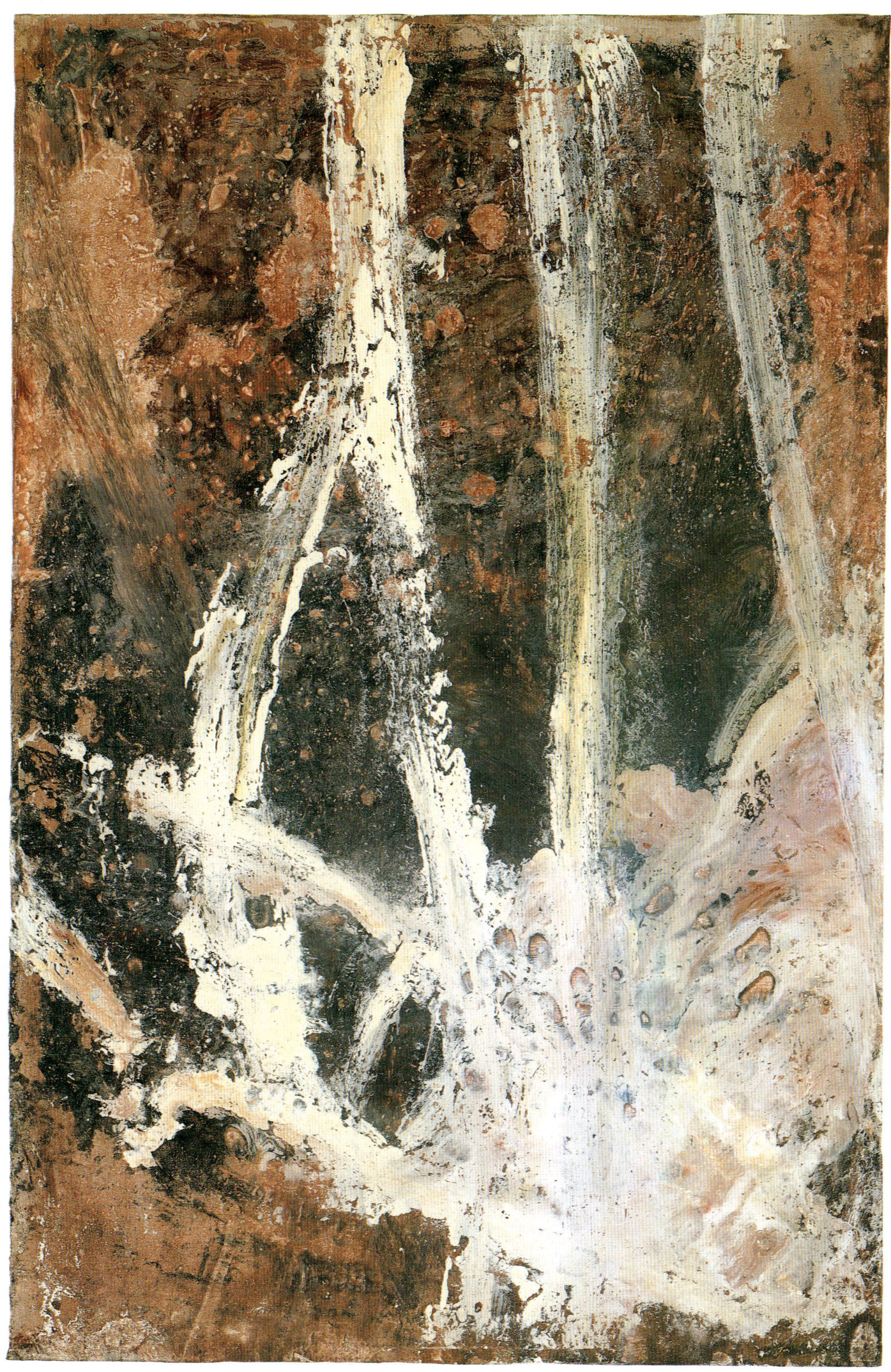

Transfer Painting 2

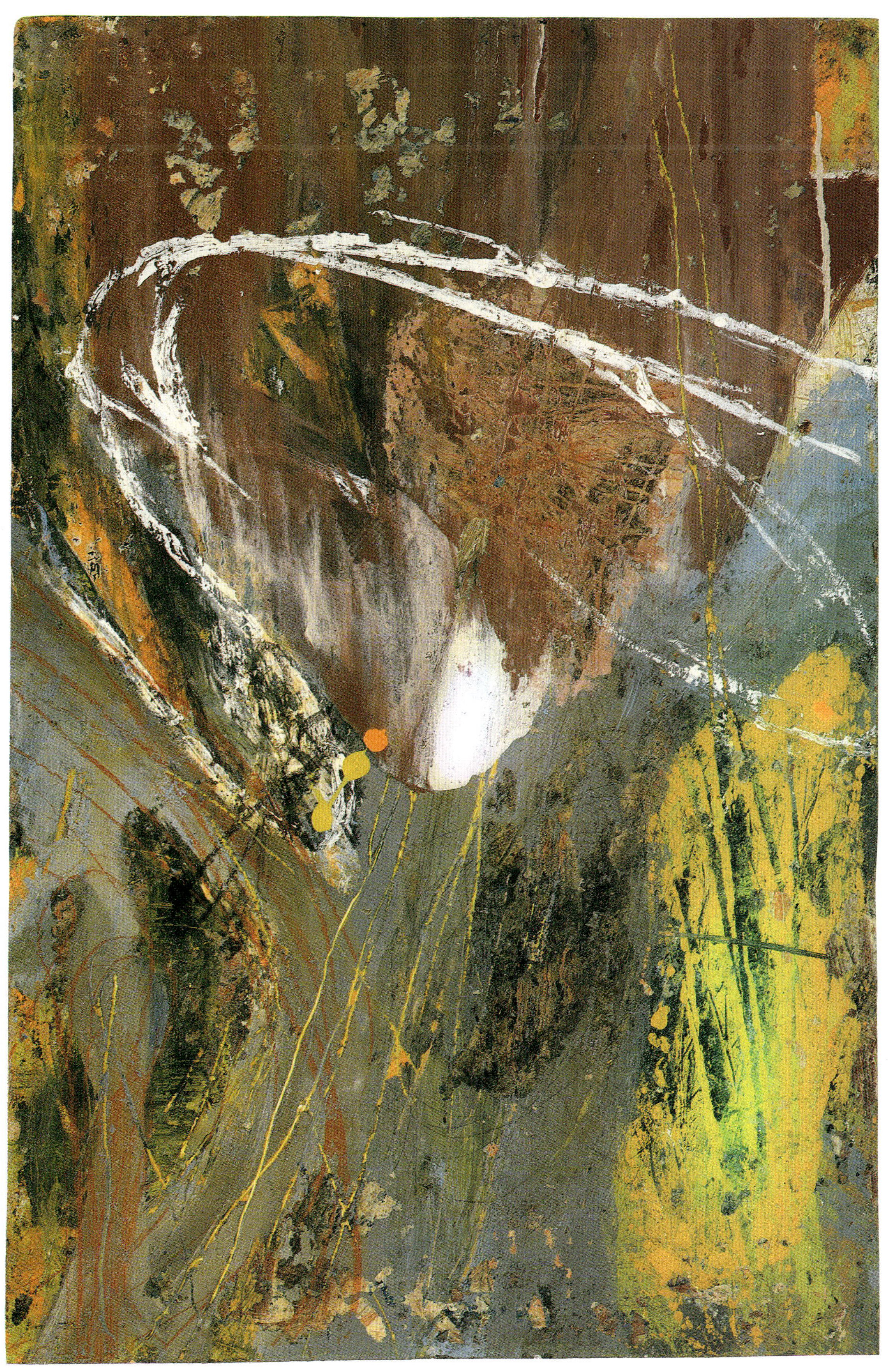

Transfer Painting 3

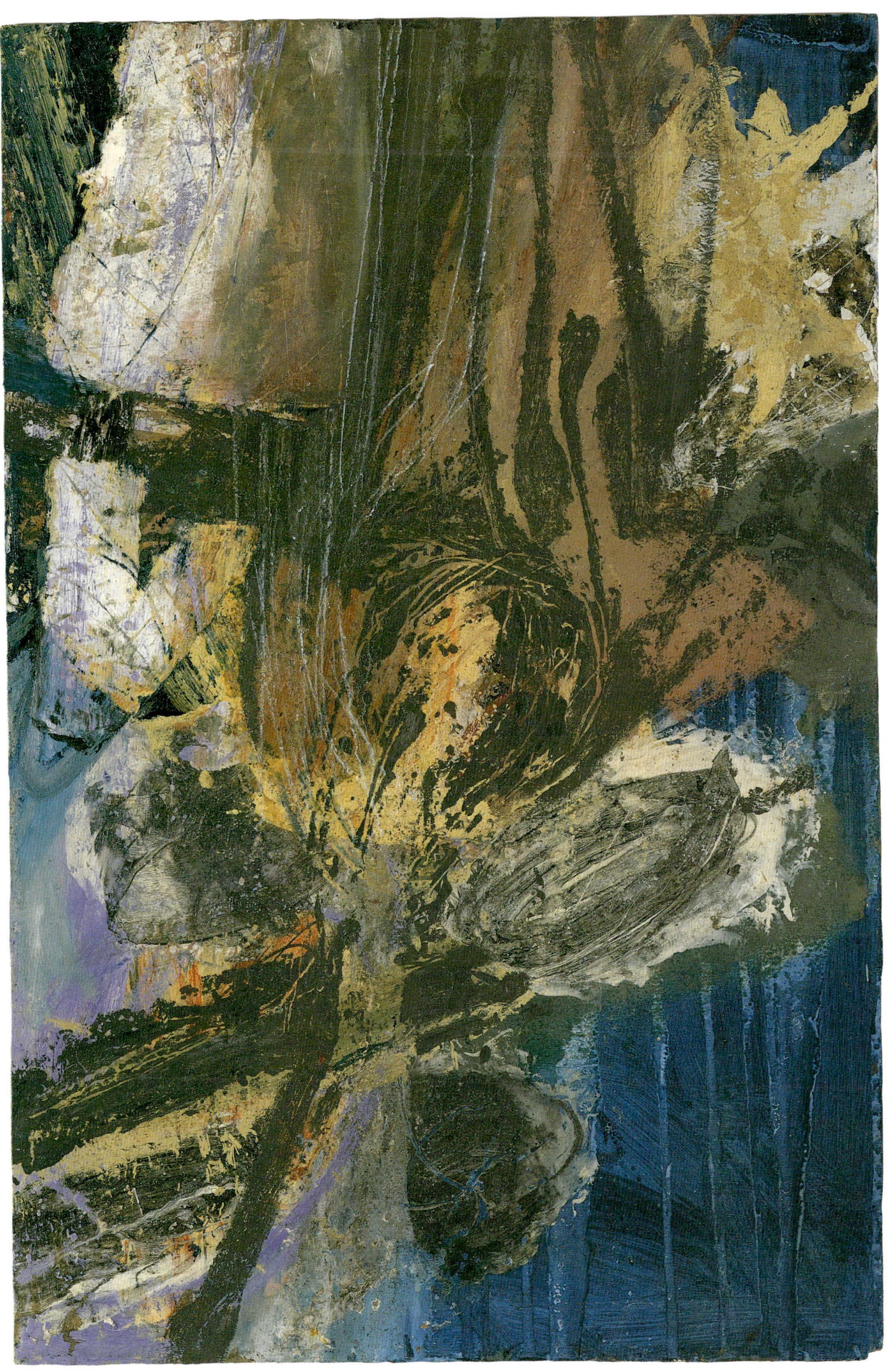

Transfer Painting 4

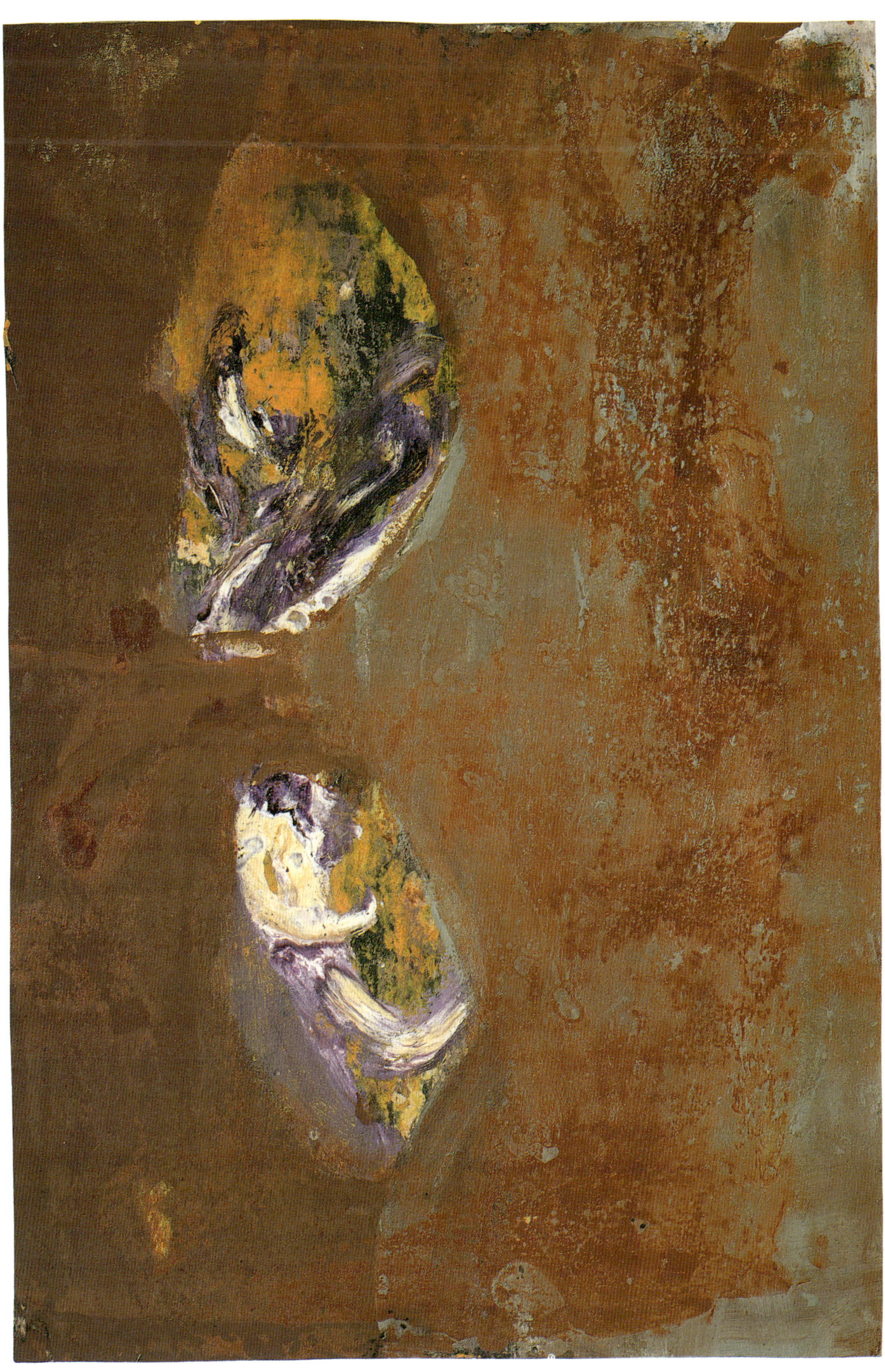

Transfer Painting 5

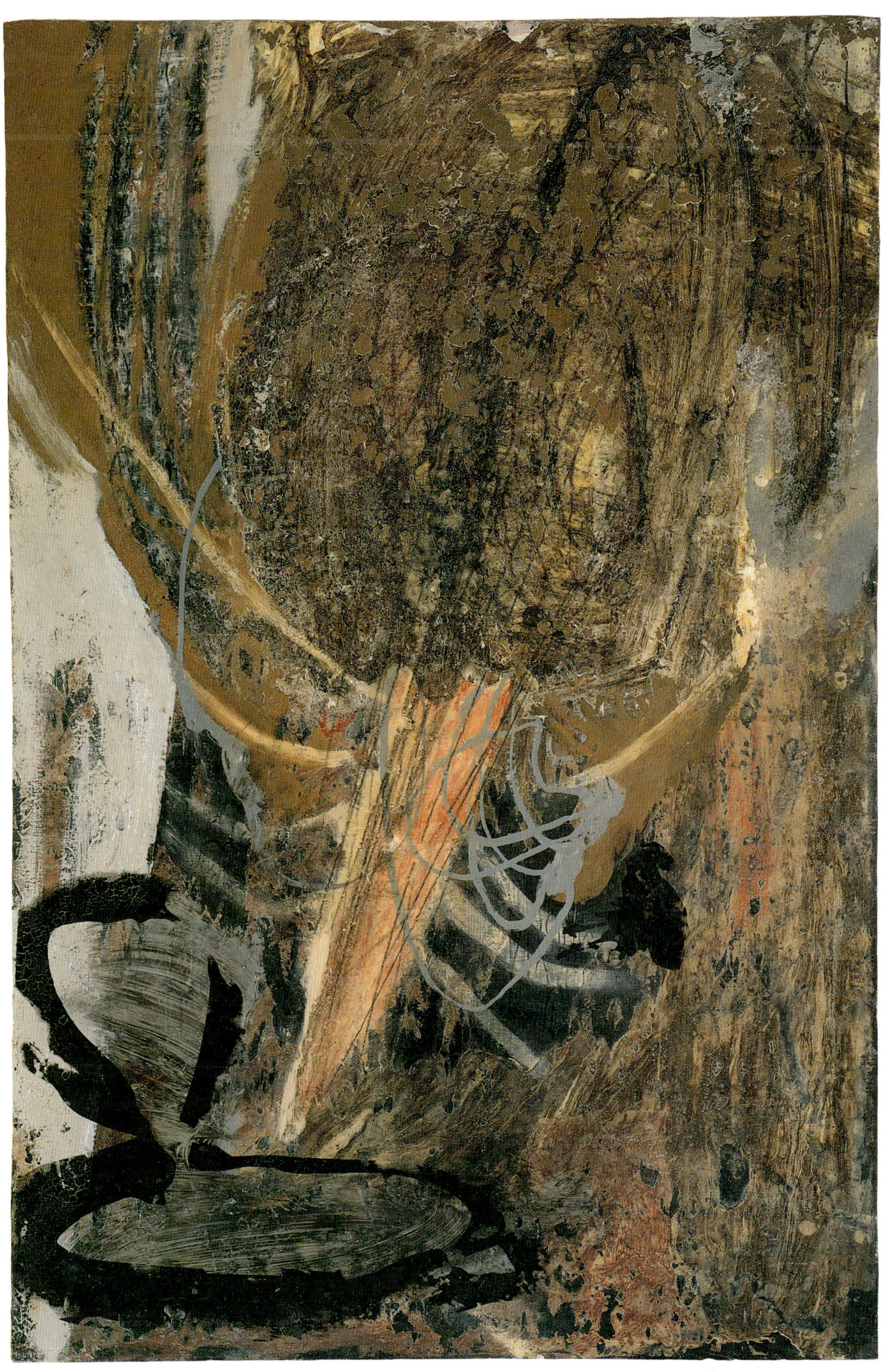

Transfer Painting 6

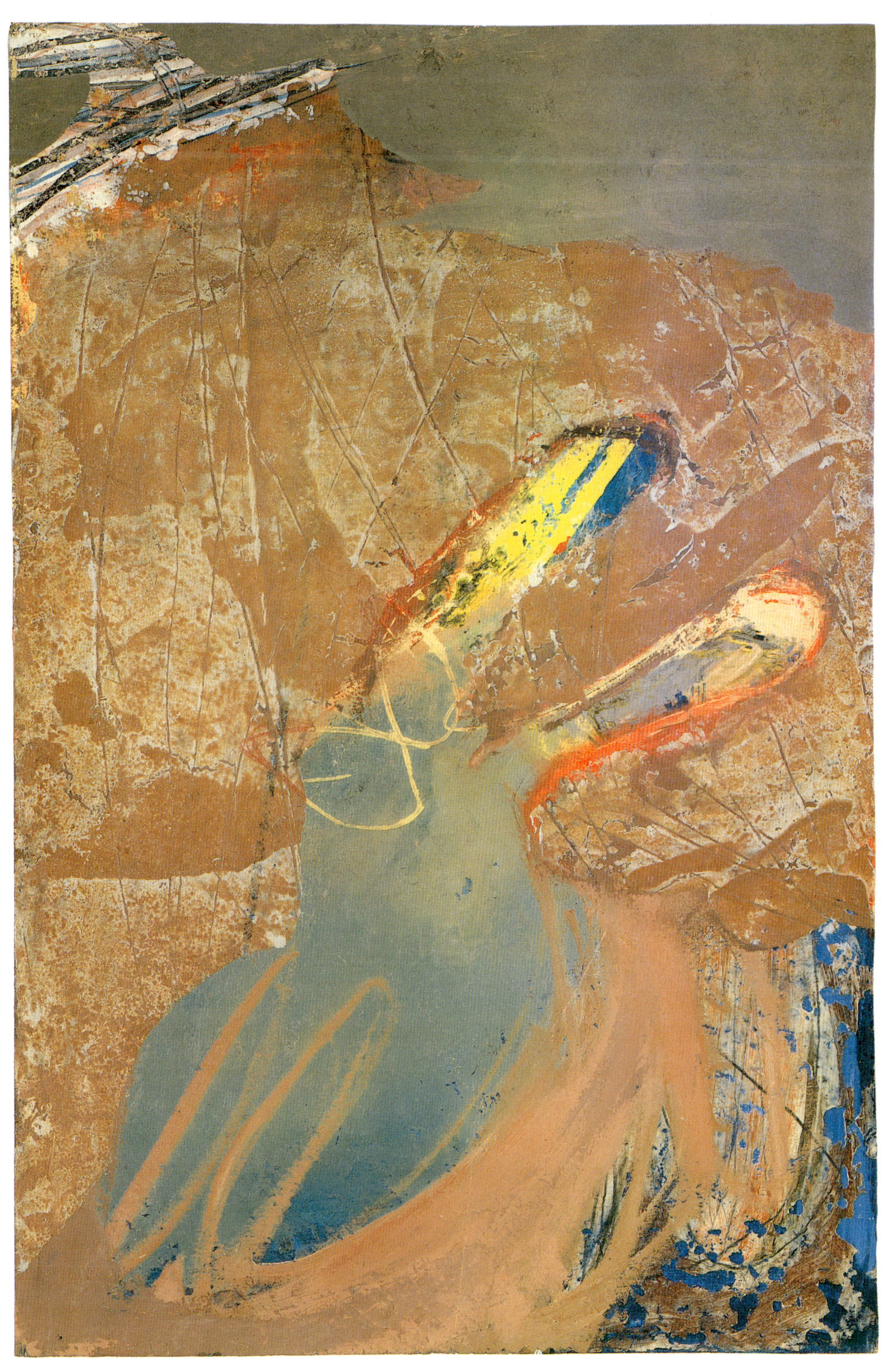

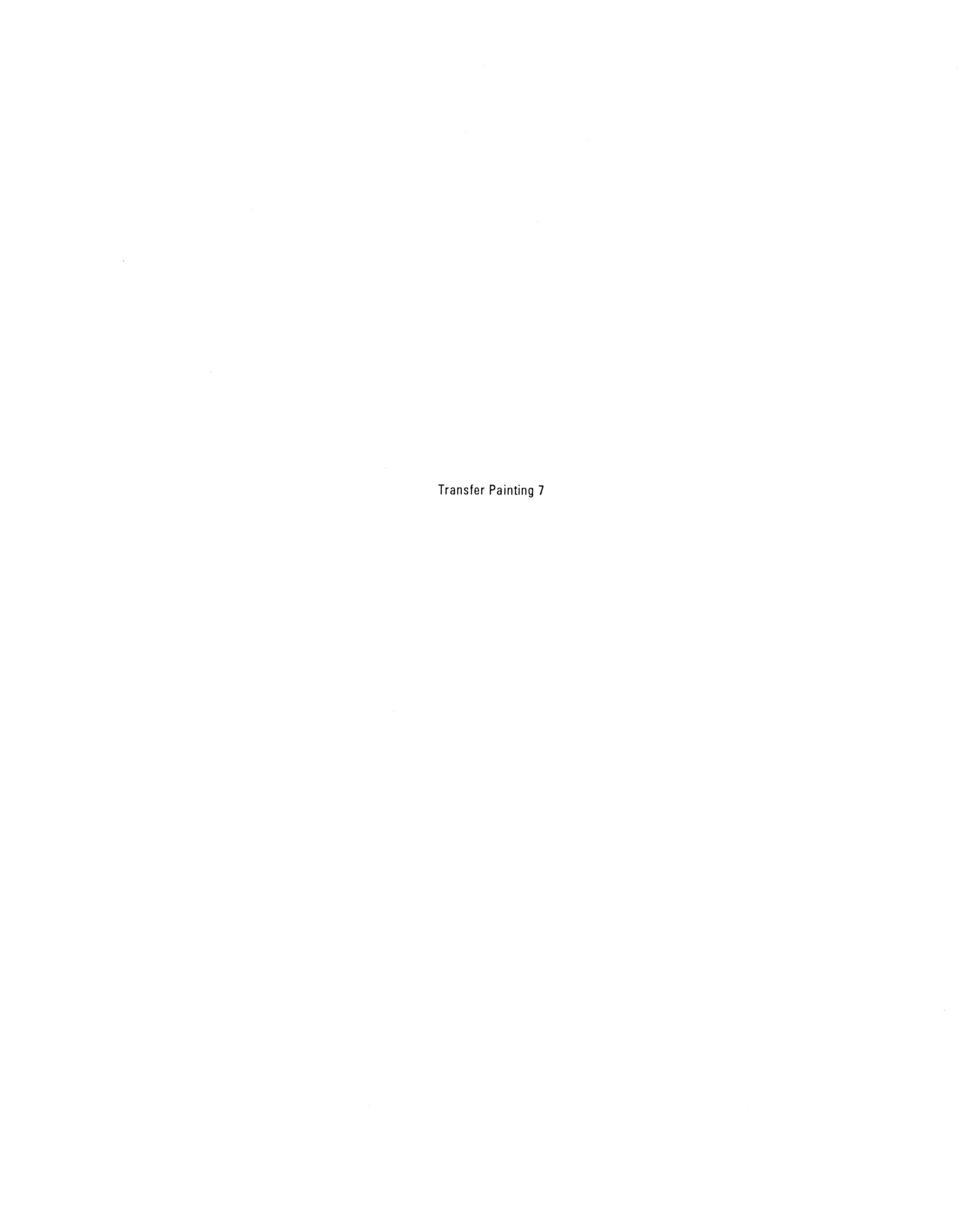

Transfer Painting 7

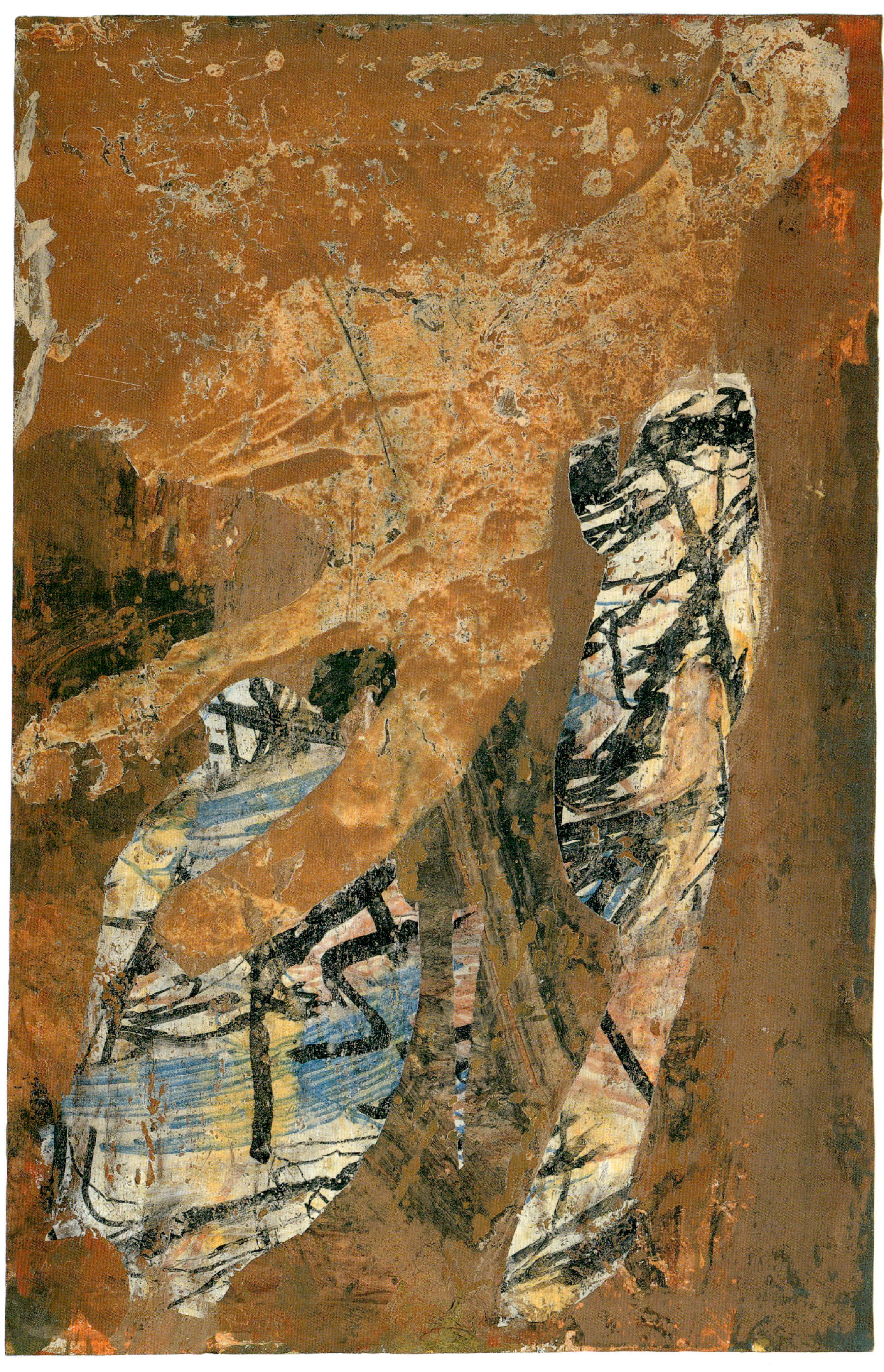

Transfer Painting 8

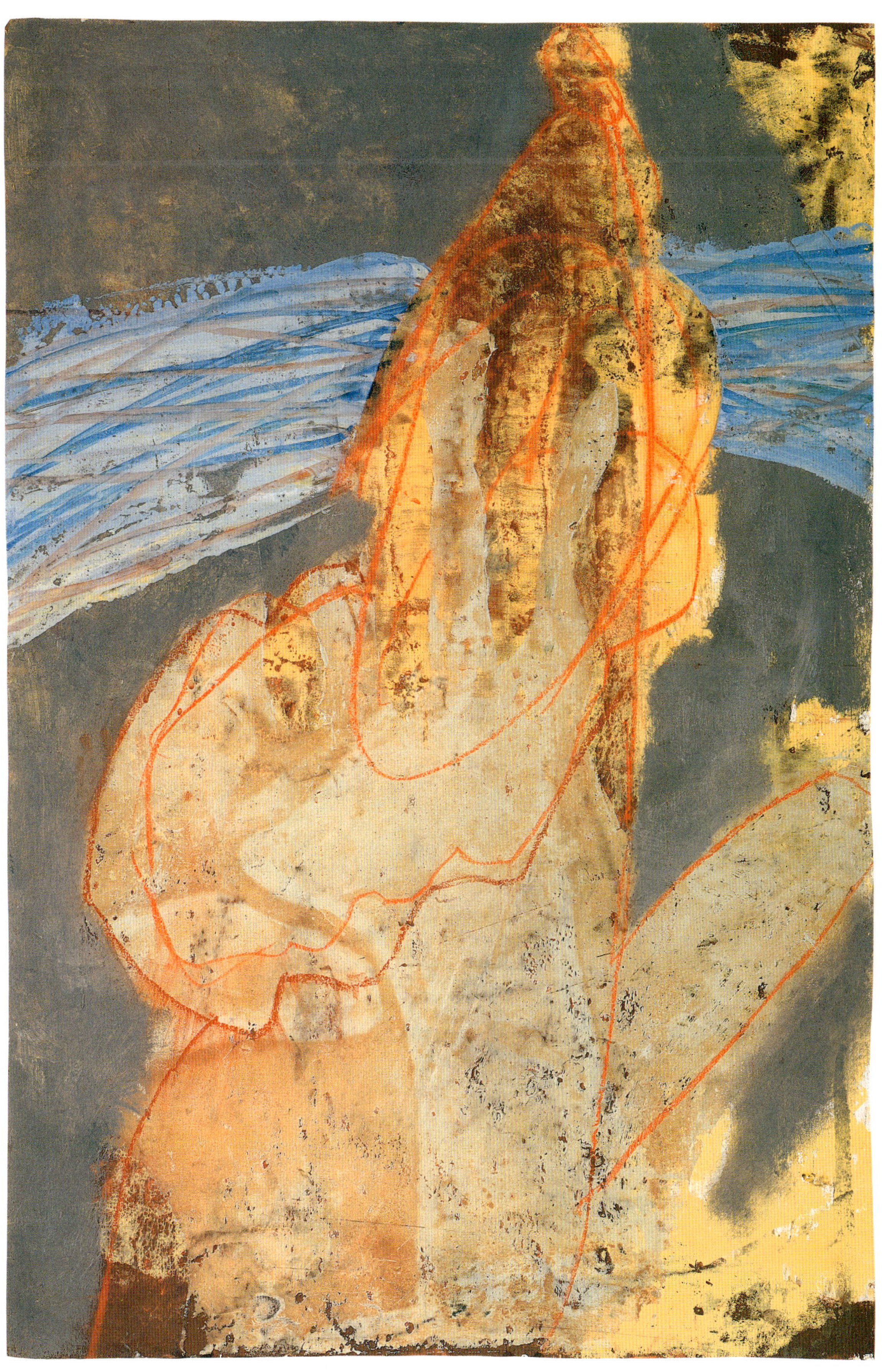

Transfer Painting 9

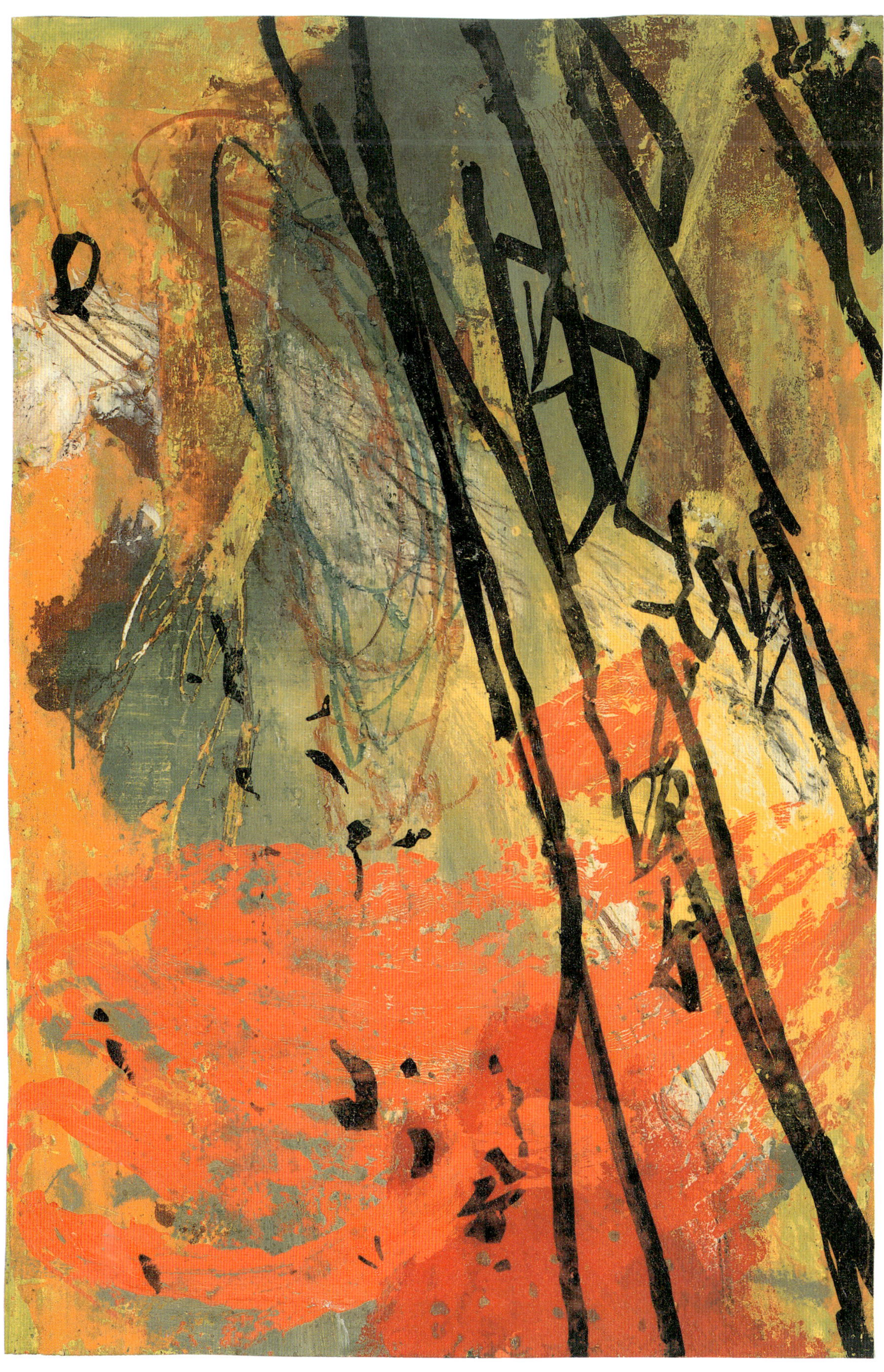

Transfer Painting 10

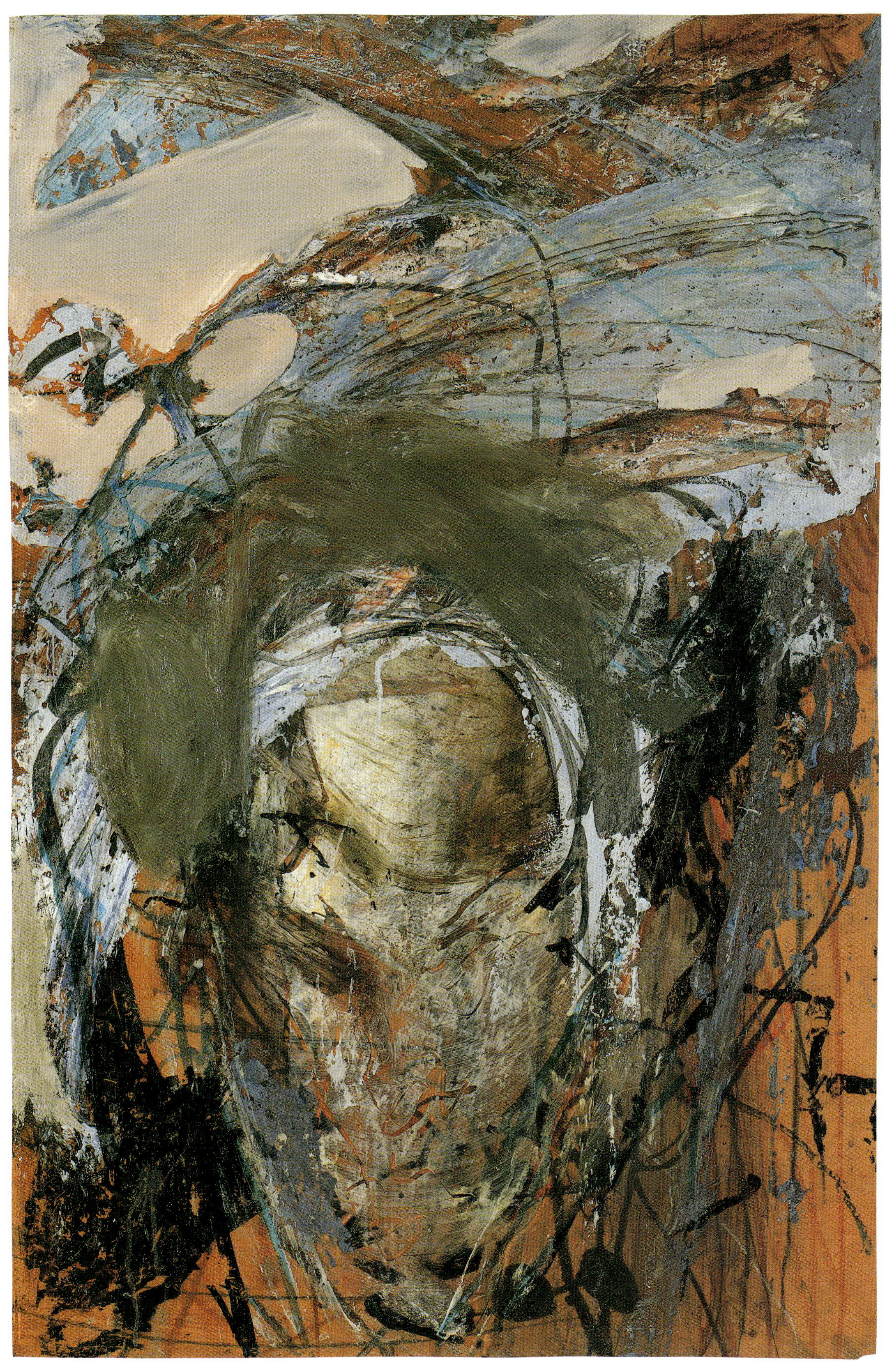

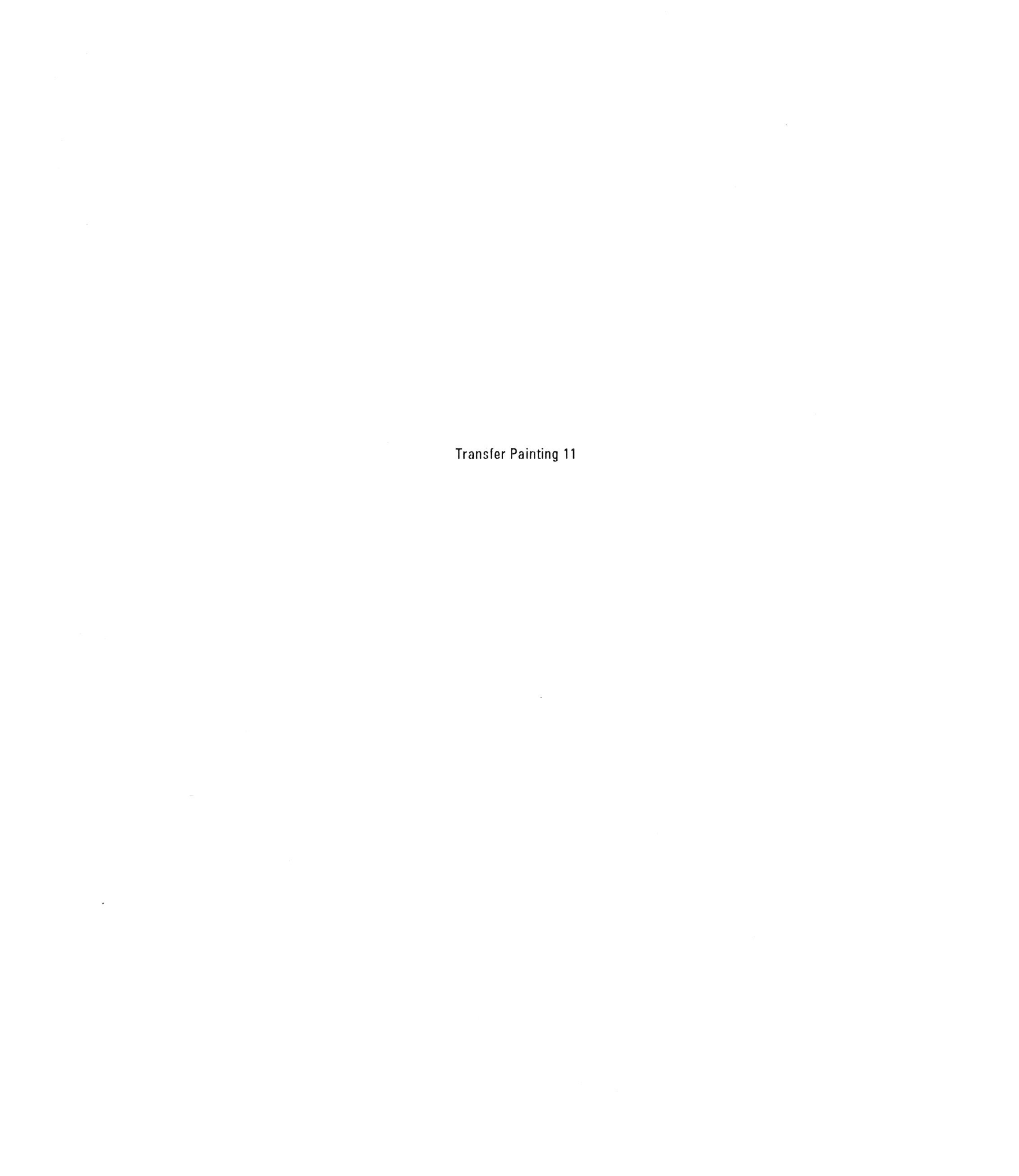

Transfer Painting 11

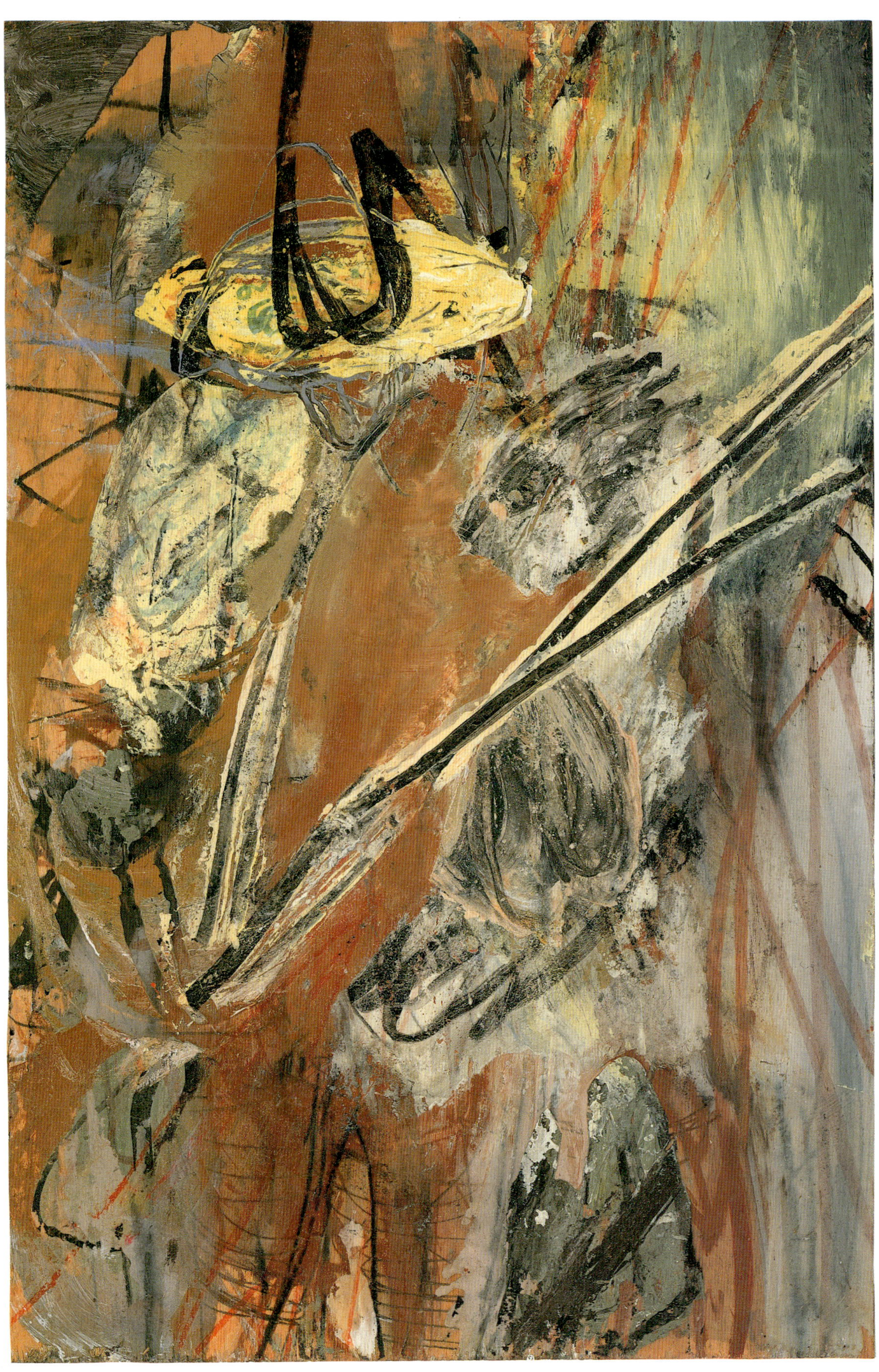

Transfer Painting 12

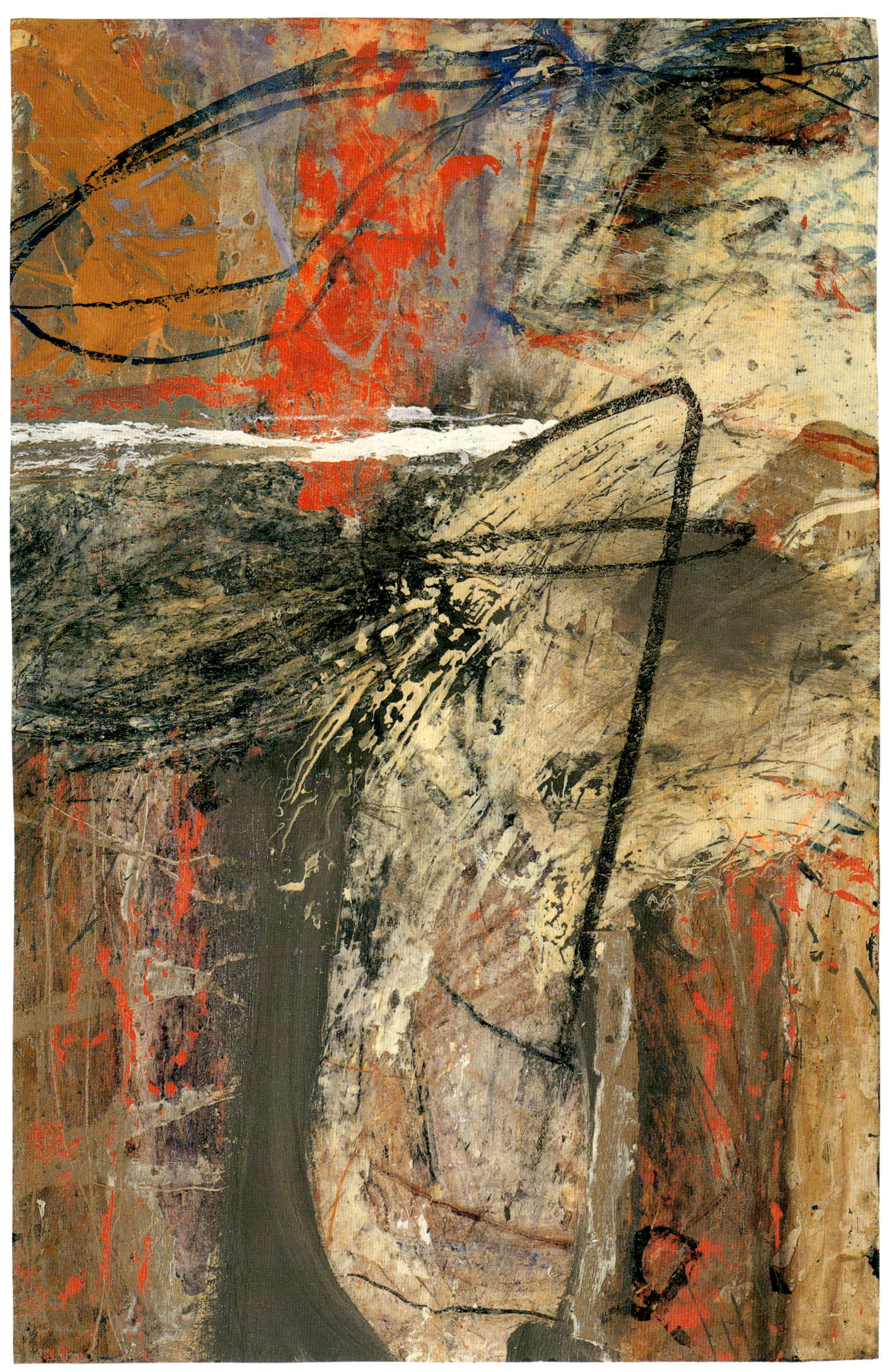

Transfer Painting 13

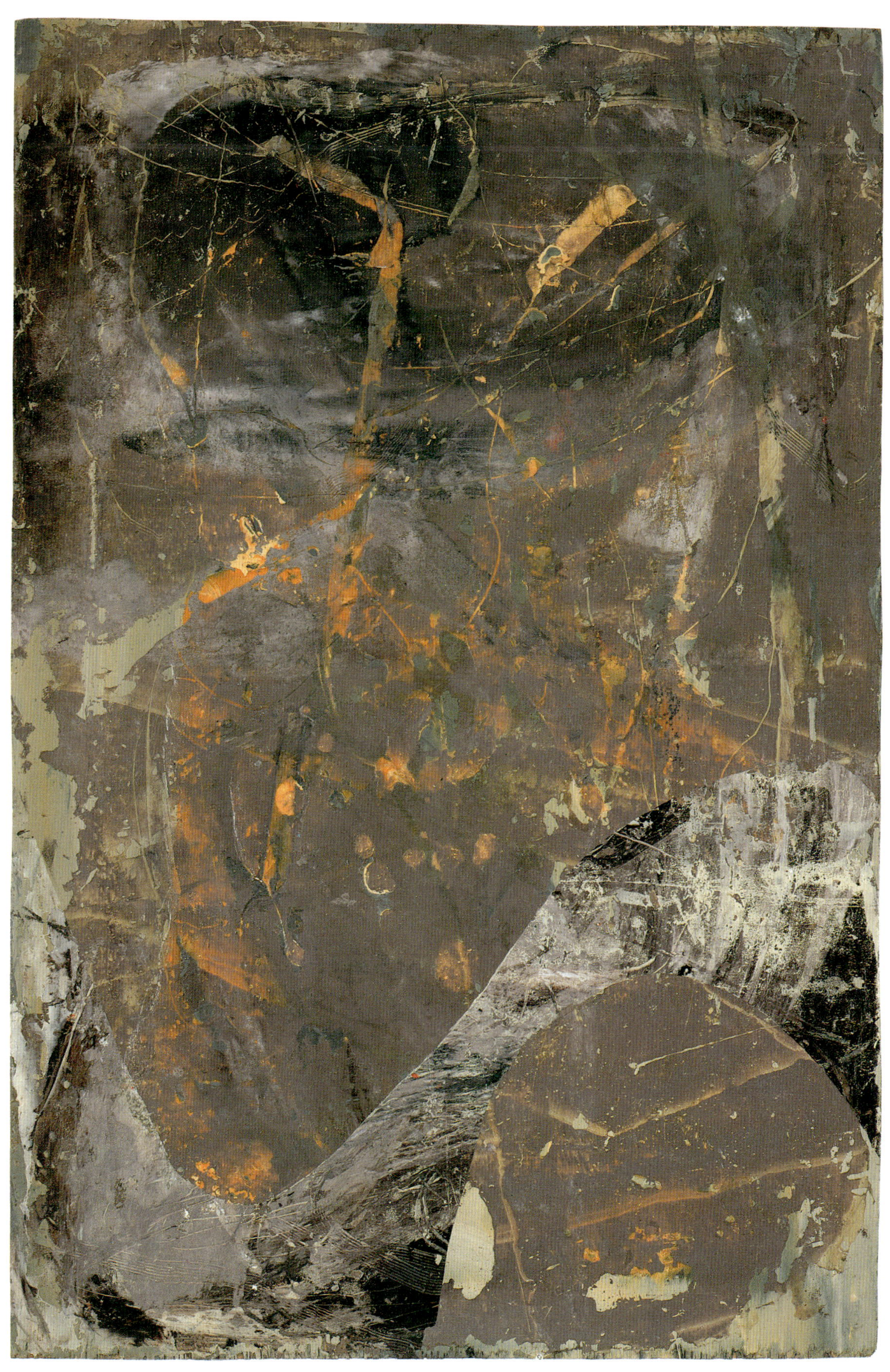

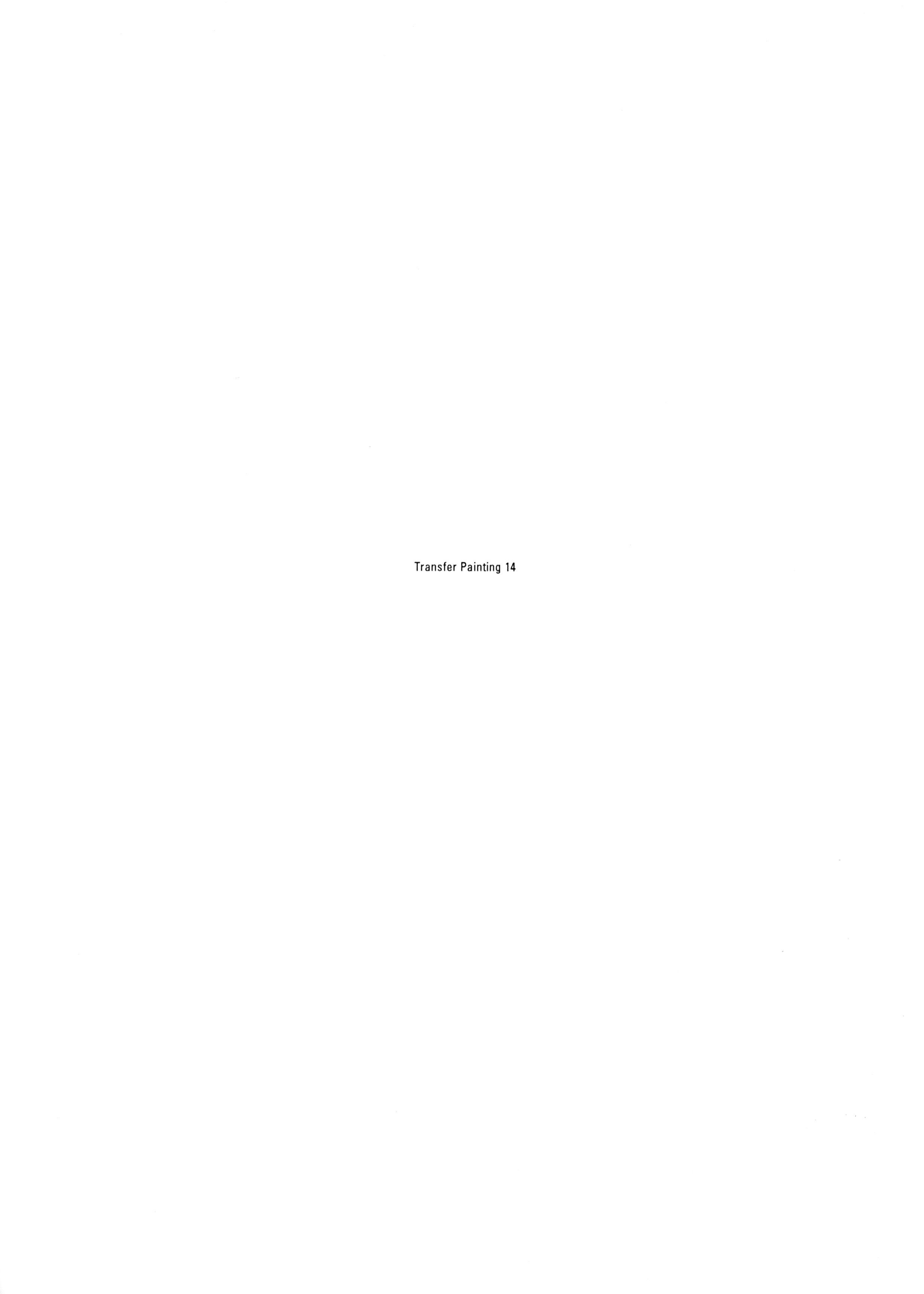

Transfer Painting 14

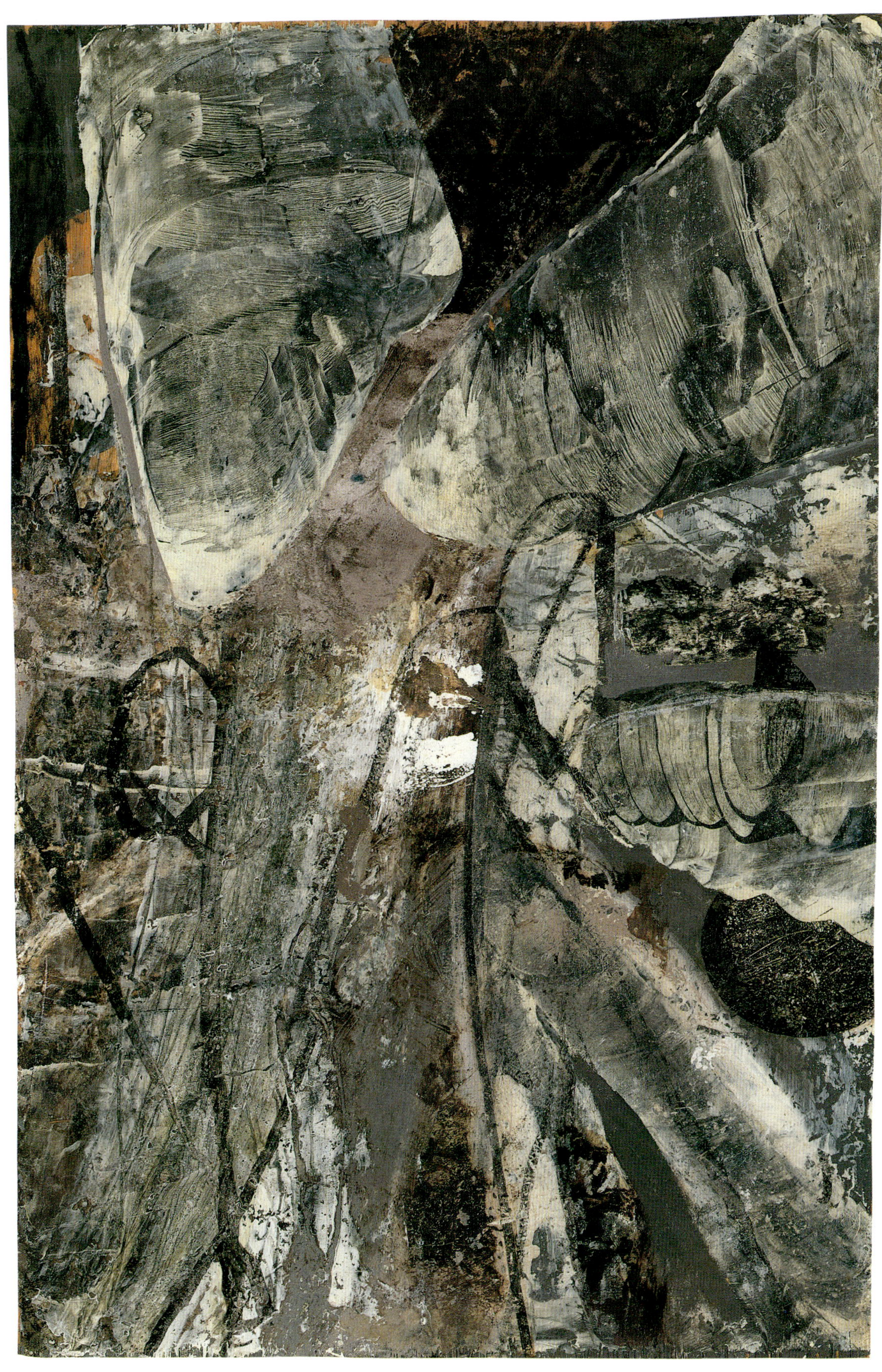

Transfer Painting 15

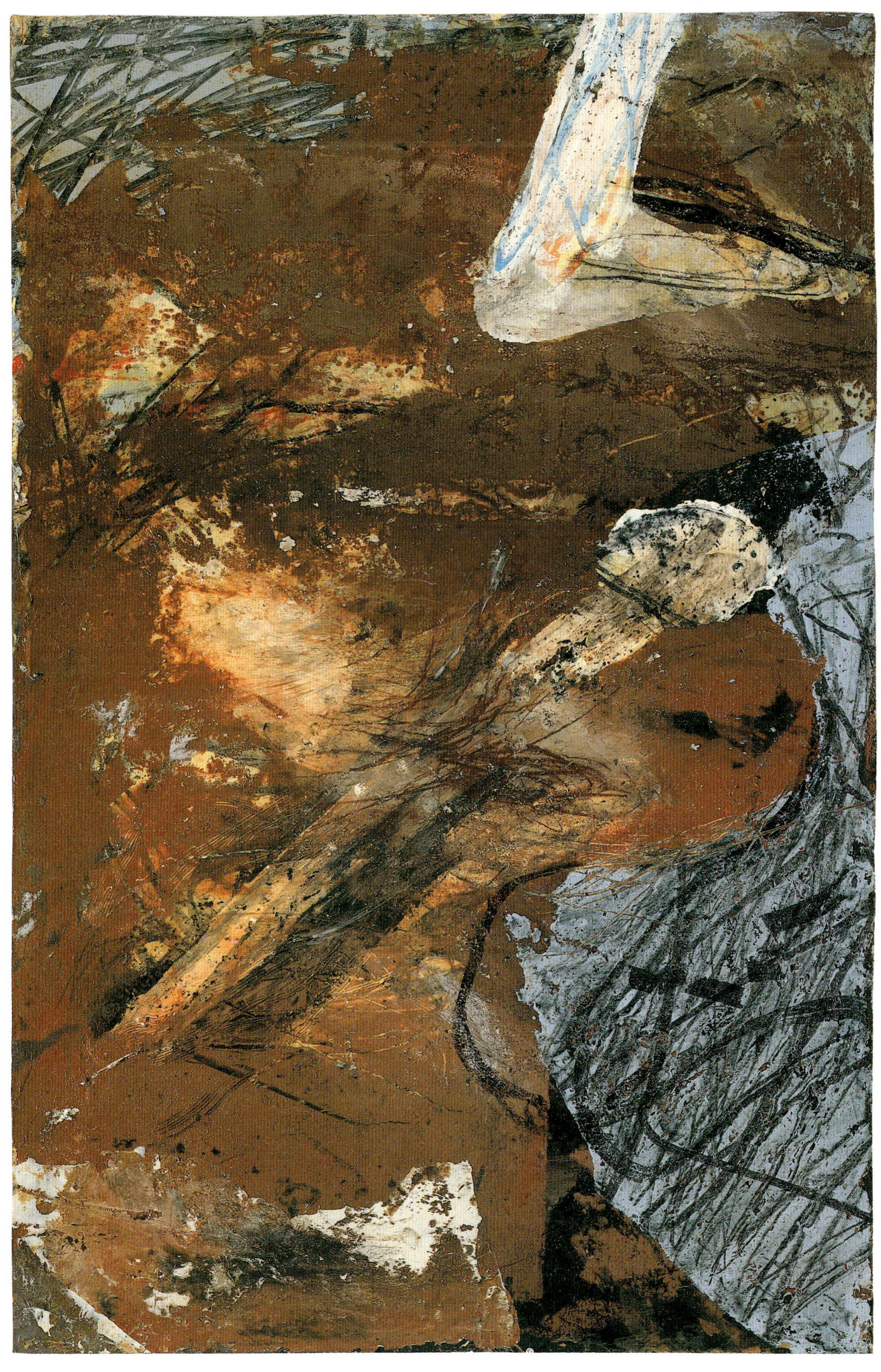

Adam Lowe

Born 1959

1978-81   Ruskin School of Art, Oxford

1982-85   Royal College of Art

One Man Shows

1986	Smith's Gallery, London, organised by Richard Pomeroy
1989	Pomeroy Purdy Gallery, London
1990	Eastbourne Clark Gallery, Florida
1990	Pomeroy Purdy Gallery, London, 'Las Frutas' (launch of a limited edition boxed set of prints)
1991	The Transfer Paintings, Pomeroy Purdy Gallery, London

Group Shows

1980	Ceramics, Somerville College, Oxford
1981	Selection from 1981 Degree Shows, Morley Gallery, London
1982	Young Figurative Painters, Fieldbourne Gallery, London
1984	Five Painters from the Royal College of Art, Consort Gallery, Imperial College, London
	Smith's Gallery, organised by Richard Pomeroy
1985	Royal College of Art Degree Show
	Prelude, Kettles Yard, Cambridge
	85 Show, Serpentine Gallery, London
1986	Leicester Schools Exhibition, Beaumont Hall, Leicester
	One Year On, ICA Fair, Olympia, London
	Young Masters, Solomon Gallery, London
	Six Artists, Groucho Club, Soho
1987	Opening Show, Richard Pomeroy Gallery
	A Printed Image, Richard Pomeroy Gallery
1988	Summer Show, Pomeroy Purdy Gallery
	Print Show, Pomeroy Purdy Gallery
1989	Blasphemies, Ecstacies, Cries, curated by Andrew Brighton, The Serpentine Gallery, London
	School of London, Odette Gilbert Gallery
1990	New Work by Gallery Artists, Pomeroy Purdy Gallery
	Group Show, Colegio De Arquitectos of Malaga, Spain, with Tony Bevan,
	Glenys Johnson and Joao Penalva, curated by Enrique Juncosa